THE BELLES HEURES OF JEAN, DUKE OF BERRY

THE BELLES HEURES
OF JEAN, DUKE OF BERRY
PRINCE OF FRANCE

With an Introduction by JAMES J. RORIMER

AT THE CLOISTERS · THE METROPOLITAN
MUSEUM OF ART · NEW YORK · MCMLVIII

Published by The Metropolitan Museum of Art, New York

All rights reserved, 1958

Library of Congress Catalog Card Number 58–14149

Color reproductions printed in France by Draeger Frères; text printed in New York by The Spiral Press with ornaments adapted from the manuscript by Fritz Kredel; cover paper printed by the Meriden Gravure Co.; binding by Russell-Rutter Company.

INTRODUCTION

 The Belles Heures, from which the *ex libris* and thirty-two illuminations are here reproduced in facsimile, is one of the celebrated Books of Hours created in the second decade of the fifteenth century for Jean, Duke of Berry, prince of France (1340–1416). Like the well-known Très Riches Heures, also made for the duke and now in the Musée Condé in Chantilly, it is a rich compendium of brilliant small paintings and ranks among the great masterpieces of the Middle Ages.

The Duke of Berry, son of King John the Good and brother of Charles V and of Philip the Bold of Burgundy, lived during unsettled times. France was still suffering from the ravages of the Black Death. The invasions and deprivations of the Hundred Years' War, in spite of a thirty-five-year lull, had weakened and disrupted the country. Internal rebellion and popular revolt against unendurable taxes created constant ferment. Charles VI's periodic fits of lunacy exposed the crown to contention, and the disunity stemming from the rivalry of the Burgundians and the Armagnacs divided France and contributed to her defeat by the English at Agincourt.

Still, the Duke of Berry built twenty castles and surrounded his luxurious court with the most illustrious artists and artisans of his time. As a patron of the arts he formed one of the largest and most varied collections in history. His passion for commissioning and collecting manuscripts was renowned. In this field, as in others, he has had few rivals.

Before the invention of the printing press extended the written word far beyond the limits of the especially privileged, only royalty, the nobility, and the Church could afford fine books. Handsomely illuminated Books of Hours were not regarded as everyday prayer books whose pages could be turned endlessly and replaced when worn out. The parchment pages of the Belles Heures, with their attractively colored scenes and designs, have been preserved in virtually pristine condition by loving care throughout the ages. Following the death of the duke our volume was purchased by Yolande of Aragon, Queen of Sicily and Duchess of Anjou. In 1954 it was acquired by the Museum for The Cloisters, with funds provided by John D. Rockefeller, Jr., from Baron Maurice de Rothschild.

The *ex libris* of the manuscript by the duke's secretary Flamel states that it was made for Jean of Berry. The duke's escutcheon, the golden fleurs-de-lis of France on an azure ground within an indented red border, appears on five pages; three display his emblems, the bear and the swan, which also may be seen among the marginal scrolls of the Annunciation scene. His motto "le temps venra" appears in the calendar for December.

Many artists were called to the court of Jean of Berry, but existing documents do not reveal the names of the illuminators of the Belles Heures. Scholars attribute the illustrations in the manuscript to Pol de Limbourg and his brothers, Herman and Jean, and perhaps their co-workers. There can be no doubt of the close relationship in style between our manuscript and many of the illustrations in the Très Riches Heures in Chantilly, which is known to be the work of the Limbourg brothers. In the inventories of the duke's manuscripts made after his death, the Très Riches Heures is entered as "Item, in a portfolio, many sections of a very rich Hours which Pol and his brothers made, very richly illustrated and illuminated." Among other indications of the close relationship between Pol and the duke are the payments he received in 1413 "in consideration of the good and agreeable services which [he] gave to Monseigneur every day." There is evidence that he was employed at the court of the Duke of Berry by 1409. In 1402 Pol and Jean de Limbourg were working for Philip the Bold of Burgundy, who died in 1404.

The pages of such books as the Chantilly Hours and our own demanded extraordinary and painstaking devotion. The former, we know, was the labor of several artists working in association. It was begun about 1413 and was not completed at the time of the duke's death in 1416. The Belles Heures, except for one unfinished page, was apparently produced between about 1410 and the time of its listing as a bound volume in 1413.

The book is divided into a number of parts. It begins with the calendar, followed by scenes from the life of Saint Catherine and the Evangelists. Then come the Hours of the Virgin, followed by several short sections: the penitential psalms, litanies, the Hours of the Cross, the Hours of the Holy Spirit, miscellaneous prayers, the history of Saint Bruno, and the founding of the Chartreuse. The later divisions are the Office of the Dead, the Hours of the Passion, the suffrages of the saints and the history of Heraclius, and Masses preceded by lives of saints. The book ends with a prayer for travel.

Many matters pertinent to the manuscript, detailed descriptions of the illuminations and considerations of style and attribution, are published elsewhere. When the Belles Heures, also known as the Heures d'Ailly, was acquired from the Ailly family in 1880 by Baron Edmond de Rothschild (from whose collection it came into the possession of Baron Maurice de Rothschild), Léopold Delisle in *Melanges de paléographie et de bibliographie* identified it in the Duke of Berry's inventories of 1413 and 1416, where it is listed as a "belles heures, very well and richly illustrated." Fifty years ago Paul Durrieu, in an article in the *Gazette des Beaux-Arts* regretted that the manuscript was not better known. As recently as 1953 the Bibliothèque Nationale published *Les Belles Heures de Jean de France* with reproductions of all the pictures and an admirable text by Jean Porcher, Curator of Manuscripts. Also in 1953 Professor Erwin Panofsky in his monumental *Early Netherlandish Painting* prepared the way for further study by proposing its historical and stylistic place.

Margaret B. Freeman, who has provided the notes for the illustrations that follow, wrote a lively account of the problem in the Museum *Bulletin* for December 1956.

It is hoped that the 33 reproductions included here—only a token selection from the 94 full-page and the 54 column illuminations, the 24 medallions in the calendar, and the marginal vignettes decorating the 224 folios—will be one of a series of color reproductions that will afford a wide public a better knowledge of this jewel among great Gothic manuscripts. The pages of the manuscript measure 6⅝ by 9⅜ inches. The reproductions, engraved and printed by Draeger Frères, France, lack small portions of the margins of the inner borders that could not be photographed without removing the tooled and stamped leather binding of the book, which was considered inadvisable. This is an early seventeenth-century replacement of the original red velvet binding with gold clasps bearing the arms of the duke, described in an inventory of his treasures made in 1413.

Frederick B. Adams, Jr., Director of the Pierpont Morgan Library, members of his staff, and Professor Millard Meiss of Harvard University gave considerable encouragement and advice when the acquisition of this manuscript for The Cloisters was first being considered.

JAMES J. RORIMER, DIRECTOR

EX LIBRIS OF JEAN, DUKE OF BERRY Translated, this inscription reads: "These Hours were made to the order of the very excellent and mighty Prince Jehan, son of the King of France, Duke of Berry and Auvergne, Count of Poitou, Etampes, Boulogne, and Auvergne. Flamel." Jean Flamel was the duke's secretary. Folio 1.

es fleurs. fist faire. Tr

xcellent et puissant prince Jehan

fils de Roy de France. Duc de Berry

Et d'auvergne Conte de Poitou et estampes

De Boulomgne Et d'auvergne Lamel.

DESCRIPTION OF THE PLATES

by Margaret B. Freeman, *Curator of The Cloisters*

 1 ANNUNCIATION In medieval Books of Hours the Annunciation scene almost always introduces the Hours of the Virgin and, as here, often receives special decorative treatment. The elaborate border, showing strong Italian influence, is unique in this manuscript. The Duke of Berry's coat of arms—gold fleurs-de-lis on an azure ground within an indented red border—appears in two places; the duke's emblems, the bear and the swan, can be seen as tiny figures among the leaves. In the Annunciation scene itself, the Virgin crosses her hands on her breast in a gesture of humility that seems to be derived from Italian prototypes, while an Italianate Gabriel carries the sheaf of lilies, which northern artists usually represent as a bouquet in a vase. The statuette of Moses surmounting the Virgin's reading desk represents the Old Law, as the Annunciation represents the New Law. For the office of matins. Folio 30.

2 NATIVITY Italian influence is shown here in the depiction of the shepherds so close to the manger and in the position of Joseph, seated on the ground with his head supported by his hand. The wattle fence, the fire, and the pot for cooking are all characteristic of northern representations of the Nativity. For the office of prime in the Hours of the Virgin. Folio 48 verso.

3 ANNUNCIATION TO THE SHEPHERDS

The Limbourg brothers painted figures in strange postures for dramatic effect. Here the attitudes of the shepherds well express their wonder at the angels, who have come so close to earth that they can almost be touched. Exquisitely drawn castles on the sky line, bearing little or no relation to the story, are found often in the manuscript. The Limbourg brothers were among the first artists to realize that distance changed the color and dimmed the outlines of objects. For the office of terce. Folio 52.

4 ADORATION OF THE MAGI

The three kings, one old, one middle-aged, and the other young, represent the three ages of man. All three royal visitors have removed their crowns in the presence of a King who, though in lowly surroundings, is greater than they. Italian influence is shown in the combining of the nativity scene, the shepherds, and the Magi. In the distance stands an idol that will fall from its pedestal when the Holy Family flees into Egypt. For the office of sext in the Hours of the Virgin. Folio 54 verso.

5 FLIGHT INTO EGYPT

Joseph, with his crumpled boots and dour look, contrasts with the warm and tender Virgin, who shields her Child in a voluminous, brilliant blue cloak. The sky, as in many other landscapes of this manuscript, suggests limitless space, an unusual accomplishment for the period. In accordance with apocryphal stories, pagan idols are shown falling at the approach of the Holy Family. This composition may have been inspired by the wing of an altarpiece by the Flemish painter Melchior Broederlam in Dijon, made about 1394 for the Duke of Berry's brother, Philip of Burgundy. For the office of compline in the Hours of the Virgin. Folio 63.

6 KISS OF JUDAS This is one of three illustrations for matins of the Hours of the Passion. It follows the accounts given in the Gospels: the betrayal of the Master by Judas' kiss, the cutting off of Malchus' ear by the impetuous Peter, and the healing of the wound by a touch of Christ's hand. The Limbourg brothers, like many other artists of the time, have shown a lantern held high to indicate that the event occurred at night. For the office of matins in the Hours of the Passion. Folio 123 verso.

7 DELIVERANCE OF BARABBAS At the feast of Passover Pilate was accustomed to "release unto the people a prisoner, whom they would." One prisoner, called Barabbas, had committed murder in an insurrection. Pilate offered to free either Jesus or Barabbas. The people, instigated by the chief priests, chose Barabbas. (Matthew 27: 15–21.) For the office of prime in the Hours of the Passion. Folio 136.

8 DARKNESS AT THE CRUCIFIXION "Now from the sixth hour there was darkness over all the land unto the ninth hour . . . and the earth did quake, and the rocks rent; and the graves were opened, and many bodies of the saints which slept arose." (Matthew 27: 45–52.) This illustration is one of the rare "night" scenes in medieval art. For the office of none in the Hours of the Passion. Folio 145 verso.

9 DESCENT FROM THE CROSS "When the even was come . . . Joseph of Arimathaea, an honorable counselor . . . went in boldly unto Pilate, and craved the body of Jesus." And Pilate assented. Then Joseph "brought fine linen, and took him down." (Mark 15: 43–46.) The thirteenth-century mystic Pseudo-Bonaventura, in his *Meditations*, says that when the nails were drawn out, John quietly made a sign to Nicodemus to hide them from the Virgin; then "Our Lady

taketh in to her hands reverently Our Lord's right hand and . . . kisseth it." For the office of vespers of the Hours of the Passion. Folio 149.

10 LAMENTATION The scene of lamentation is not described in the Bible. However, many medieval artists depict this interlude between the Descent and the Entombment. Pseudo-Bonaventura says that the Mother took her Son's head and shoulders to her breast, Mary Magdalen kissed his feet, and others "of the company stood about . . . all making great lamentation." The kneeling Mary Magdalen and the mourning woman tearing her hair recall figures from Giottesque paintings. For vespers of the Hours of the Passion. Folio 149 verso.

11 THE COURT OF HEAVEN This is the illustration for the Mass of All Saints' Day. In the center the Virgin and Child in glory are surrounded by seraphim and adoring saints. Among the saints are Peter, in a white robe, and Paul, in a heliotrope-colored cloak carrying a sword. Below are Dorothea with a basket of flowers, Catherine with a wheel, Margaret with a dragon, Barbara with a tower, and either Saint Agatha or Saint Apollonia with pincers. Above, God the Father is flanked by Saint John the Baptist and Saint John the Evangelist and surrounded by seraphim. This unusual composition of the court of heaven was probably derived, as Jean Porcher has pointed out, from a Paris manuscript dated 1405, now in the Bibliothèque Nationale. Folio 218.

12 STORY OF SAINT CATHERINE Catherine in Prison. The Belles Heures is unusual in that it includes several profusely illustrated lives of the saints. The story of Saint Catherine in the manuscript follows in general *The Golden Legend* by Jacobus da Voragine. Catherine, the daughter of a king, beautiful and in wisdom passing all others, so enraged Emperor Maxentius by her eloquent defence of

Christianity and her refusal to become his second wife that he ordered her to be tortured and cast into a dark dungeon. But the empress had a great love for Catherine and went at night to visit her. When she arrived she saw the prison shining with great clearness and angels anointing Catherine's wounds. And before the night was over, the empress was converted to Christianity. Folio 17 verso.

13 STORY OF SAINT CATHERINE Catherine's body is carried to Mount Sinai. The emperor ordered Catherine to be broken between two wheels but an angel of the Lord smashed the wheels. Finally Maxentius commanded his executioner to smite off her head. "And when she was beheaded . . . angels took the body and bare it unto the Mount of Sinai, more than twenty [days' journey] from thence, and buried it there honorably." One hundred and thirty years later holy hermits led by an angel discovered her body; and "with great joy and reverence" they carried it down to the chapel they had previously built in her honor. And "Our Lord showed there many miracles." In this illustration medieval pilgrims are shown climbing up to the shrine. Folio 20.

14 SAINT BRUNO AND THE GRANDE CHAR-TREUSE Bruno Departing with His Students. The account in this manuscript follows for the most part the medieval Life of Saint Bruno published in the *Acta Sanctorum*. Bruno, a teacher at Rheims and most learned in philosophy and theology, was persuaded by a miraculous portent to give up worldly things and seek a hermit's life in the wilderness. Here Bruno's students say farewell as he sets out with several of his followers for the mountain regions of France. The flowerlike color scheme is typical of many of the illustrations in this manuscript. Folio 95 verso.

15 SAINT BRUNO AND THE GRANDE CHAR-
TREUSE The Dream of the Bishop of Grenoble. Saint Hugh, the
holy bishop of Grenoble, dreamed of a wild valley in the French mountains named the Chartreuse and he saw seven stars falling on the land,
illuminating it. The color scheme of brilliant reds, soft grays, and blues
is a fine foil for the more delicate color scheme of the opposite page.
Folio 96.

16 SAINT BRUNO AND THE GRANDE CHAR-
TREUSE Bruno before the Bishop of Grenoble. Bruno and his
six companions crossed many mountains until they came to Grenoble.
There they inquired of the bishop where they might find a remote place,
far from men, where they could live in peace and solitude. Then the
bishop understood the meaning of his dream and told the seven men of
the place that had been designated by the seven stars. Folio 96 verso.

17 SAINT BRUNO AND THE GRANDE CHAR-
TREUSE Bruno and His Companions Enter the Grande Chartreuse. The bishop of Grenoble led Bruno and his companions to the
wild spot, called the Chartreuse, that he had seen in his dream, and there
the seven men built the "first house of the order of Chartreux." The color
scheme here, based on the white habits of the Carthusian order, is sur-
prisingly effective. Folio 97.

18 SAINT BRUNO AND THE GRANDE CHAR-
TREUSE The Grande Chartreuse. Here "amongst the rugged
mountains" is the Grande Chartreuse as it probably appeared at the time
of the Duke of Berry. It consists of a two-storied chapel and a cloister
surrounded by individual cells, each with a pink-tiled roof and chimney.
Every monk "has his own cell" writes a twelfth-century abbot, "and in

these they work, sleep, eat." Here, three lay brothers are fishing, one with a rod and two with a net. This landscape picture is unique in the manuscript and unusual for the period. Folio 97 verso.

19 STORY OF SAINT JEROME Temptation of Saint Jerome. The account as told in this manuscript follows the story in *The Golden Legend* by Jacobus da Voragine. Jerome, a man learned in the holy scriptures, left the life of cities and went into the desert where "he suffered for Christ's sake." He slept on the bare earth, "fellow unto scorpions and wild beasts." He was often tempted by thoughts of "the carols of maidens and the embracements" of the flesh, so that he beat his breast and prayed the Lord for peace. At last, after "many weepings and tears" it seemed to him that he "was among the company of angels" and thus was his penance done. Folio 186.

20 STORY OF SAINT JEROME Jerome Heals a Lion. "On a day towards even Jerome sat with his brethren for to hear the holy lesson, and a lion came halting suddenly in to the monastery, and when the brethren saw him, anon they fled," but Jerome came toward the lion as he would come toward a guest, "and then the lion showed to him his foot being hurt." Then Jerome called his brethren to search for the wound and they found that the foot of the lion was hurt with a thorn. "Then this holy man put thereto diligent cure, and healed him, and he abode ever after as a tame beast with them." (Voragine, *The Golden Legend*.) Folio 186 verso.

21 STORY OF SAINT JEROME The Lion and the Ass. Jerome had the lion guard an ass that brought wood to the monastery, and once the lion fell asleep and merchants stole the ass. Jerome supposed that the lion had eaten the ass and made the lion carry wood as the ass had done. One day the lion saw a caravan of merchants and recognized the ass. "With a great roaring he ran on them so terribly that all the merchants fled," and he so frightened the camels by beating the earth with his tail that he drove them straight into the monastery "with all their charge and lading." (Voragine, *The Golden Legend*.) Folio 187.

22 STORY OF SAINTS ANTHONY AND PAUL THE HERMIT Anthony Goes to Seek Saint Paul.

Saint Anthony, who was a hermit in a desert, at one time "thought in himself that in the world was none so good [nor] so great an hermit as he was himself. Hereupon came to him a revelation as he slept that . . . low down in that desert was an hermit better than he, and that he ought to go and see this holy man. Anon after the next day he took his staff by which he sustained him, and began to go through that desert." (Voragine, *The Golden Legend*.)

The Limbourg brothers, like many other medieval painters, showed the Red Sea as literally red. The many-oared galley has a kind of awning over the stern. Folio 191 verso.

23 STORY OF SAINTS ANTHONY AND PAUL THE HERMIT A Centaur Guides Saint Anthony.

It happened as Saint Anthony was going through the desert "that he met a person . . . whom the fables of the poets call centaurs. And anon made tofore him the sign of the cross, and demanded of him where this holy man the hermit dwelt, and he showed to him the way on the right side, and anon vanished away from him." (Voragine, *The Golden Legend*.)

Here the centaur seems to be half goat instead of half horse. Folio 192.

24 STORY OF SAINTS ANTHONY AND PAUL THE HERMIT Anthony Buries Saint Paul. Not long after Saint Anthony had found Saint Paul in his hermitage, Paul announced to his visitor, "I shall now shortly die and shall go to Jesu Christ for to receive the crown . . . [and] thou art come hither for to bury my body." As Anthony returned through the desert to the hermitage one day "he saw the soul of Saint Paul, shining, ascend into heaven among a great company of angels." But when he came to bury the body "he was much abashed . . . for he had no instrument to make his sepulchre; then came two lions which much debonairly made a pit," and Anthony buried Paul therein. (Voragine, *The Golden Legend.*) Folio 193 verso.

25 SAINT GEORGE It fell to the lot of the king's daughter to be sacrificed to the dragon "which envenomed all the country." So she was led to the place where the dragon was, but when she was there Saint George passed by and found her weeping. "As they spake together the dragon appeared . . . and Saint George . . . drew out his sword and garnished him with the sign of the cross, and rode hardily against the dragon . . . and smote him with his spear." (Voragine, *The Golden Legend.*)

The Limbourg brothers have added new details to the familiar scene: an angel holds Saint George's helmet, and two baby dragons emerge from the cave. Folio 167.

26 SAINT EUSTACE The Lord wished to humble Eustace and so He tried him with many afflictions, as He did Job. At one time Eustace took his two children and "came to a river, and for the great abundance of water he durst not pass that river with his both sons at once, which were then young. But at the last he left one of them on the brink of the river, and bare over that other on his shoulders. . . . And when he was in the midst of the water, there came a wolf and took the child that he had borne over, and fled withal to the woods." And then "there came a great lion and bare away that other child." But herdsmen rescued both children and "nourished" them in their village. And many years later when they were grown men they were joyfully reunited with their father. (Voragine, *The Golden Legend.*) Folio 164 verso.

27 SAINT NICHOLAS It is written that "the blessed Nicholas was at the Council of Nice; and on a day, as a ship with mariners were ... perishing on the sea, they prayed and required devoutly [of] Nicholas, servant of God, saying: If those things that we have heard of thee ... be true, prove them now. And anon a man appeared in his likeness ... and then he began to help them in their exploit of the sea, and anon the tempest ceased." (Voragine, *The Golden Legend.*)

Here the Duke of Berry's illuminators have daringly attempted to paint a clearing sky after a storm. Folio 168.

28 SAINT URSULA Ursula, having gathered together eleven thousand virgins from divers realms, led them all on a pilgrimage to Rome. On their return, "all these virgins came ... to Cologne, and found that it was besieged with the Huns. And when the Huns saw them they began to run upon them with a great cry ... like wolves on sheep, and slew all this great multitude. And when they were all beheaded, they came to the blessed Ursula, and the prince of them, seeing her beauty so marvellous ... began to comfort her upon the death of the virgins, and promised ... to take her to his wife. And when she had refused him ... he shot at her an arrow, and pierced her through the body, and so accomplished her martydom." (Voragine, *The Golden Legend.*) Folio 178 verso.

29 SAINT CHARLEMAGNE "Charlemagne had all of France at his command. He conquered Spain and slew Agoulant. He overcame the King of Pavia and took his holdings. He won the Saxons hardily, through great battles and brave fightings so that they were all at his bidding, against their own wishes. And to the land where Our Lord gave his life for our salvation, he brought back Baptism and the Holy Sacrament." This is a translation of Jacques de Longuyon's description of Charlemagne as one of the Nine Heroes in his "Vows of the Peacock." In our manuscript Charlemagne is represented in the same hero-pose as the figures in the Duke of Berry's Nine Heroes tapestries at The Cloisters, and it may be that the Limbourg brothers "copied" their Charlemagne from the now-missing Charlemagne of the tapestries. An angel bears his coat of arms, half France and half Holy Roman Empire. Charlemagne was canonized in 1164 as the "powerful athlete of Christ." Folio 174.

30 DUCHESS OF BERRY IN PRAYER This is Jeanne of Boulogne, the Duke of Berry's second wife, whom he married in 1389. She is shown kneeling at her *prie-dieu*, praying to the Trinity, who are here represented as alike as triplets. The prayer is in French. Folio 91 verso.

31 DUKE OF BERRY IN PRAYER Here the duke is represented as clean-shaven, wearing his ducal robes and a chaplet of flowers. A small amount of repainting is noticeable around the head. Perhaps the original head covering was a crown, similar to the one the duchess wears, or possibly an elaborate hat according to the fashion of the day. The duke's prayer, in French, is to Our Lady. Folio 91.

32 DUKE OF BERRY ON A JOURNEY Authorities differ as to which of the figures represents the duke, the scarlet-coated figure at the right, painted at one of the times when the duke wore a beard, or the blue-coated figure in the center who has just removed his hat. This is the illustration for a prayer for safety while traveling. It is the last illustration in the book. Folio 223 verso.

ILLUMINATIONS

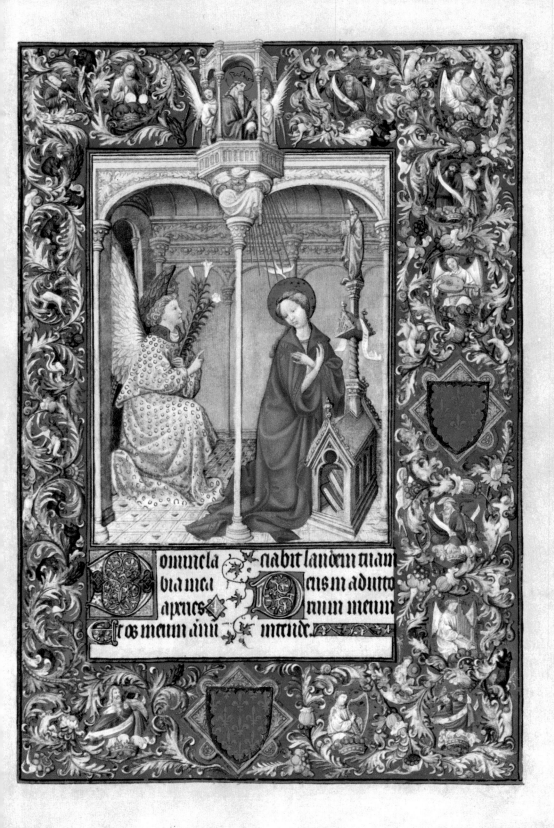

eus in ad | omine ad adui
iutorium | uandum me festina
meum in | loua pri et filio t
tende. | spiritui sancto.

eus in ad
iutorium
meum in
tende.

Domine ad adiu
uandum me festina.
Gloria patri et filio
et spiritui sancto.

Deus in ad
iutorium
meum in
tende.

Domine ad adiu
uandum me festina.
Gloria patri et filio
et spiritui sancto.

omine ad adiu
uandium me festi-
na. Gloria pri et filio
et spiritui sancto.

icut erat in prin-
cipio et nunc et sem-
per et in secula seculo-
rum. amen. Inuitato

Sicut erat in prin
apio et nunc et sem
per et in secula secu
lozum. Amen. vm.

Beata xpisti
passio sit nra
liberacio et per hanc
nobis gaudia para

eus in ad
iutorium
meum in
tende.

Domine ad adiu
uandum me festina
Gloria pri et filio et
spiritui sco.

Sicut erat in prin
apio et nunc et sem
per et in secula seculoz
Amen. ā. Miserere p̄.

Miserere mei ds
miserere mei
qm in te confidit am
ma mea.

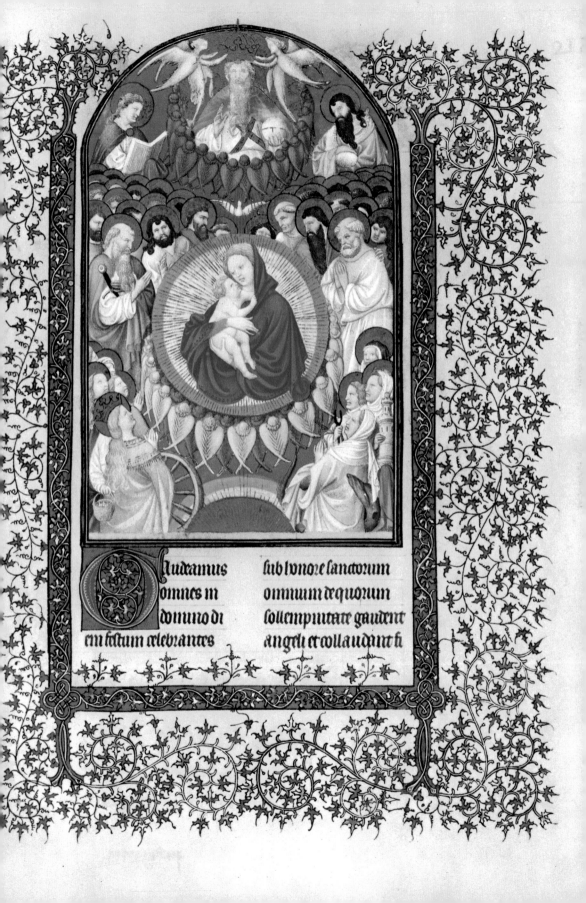

Audeamus sub honore sanctorum

omnes in omnium de quorum

domino di sollempnitate gaudent

em festum celebrantes angeli et collaudant fi

Que cum intrasset uisa in exstimabili clarita
te angelos q; plagas uiuis iungētes pro trac
to q; secum sermone usq; ad mediu nottis
dpmuys etiē uite ad xpi fidem conuersa est

Angeli aut corpus eius accipientes ab illo loco
usq; ad montē synay itīe plusq̄ dierum xi.
deduxerunt et ibi dē sepelierūt ex aū ossib;
ī del̄ in̄ctar oleū manat infirmitates sanās.

Mane facto congregatis omnibꝰ ad sepeliendū
mortuū iterū clamat. Justo dī iudico ꝛ dempnat̄
sum. vnde pterriti sunt omīs q̄ vir tante scīe
pdit̄ ēt ex quibꝰ bruno scolares suos alloquit̄.

Quid nos miseri sepius debemus exe fugiam̃ et
hiem̃us ĩ soliaidine et puem̃etes ad burgũdi
am accelerunt quẽdã epm̃ scẽ uite qui uenie
tes m sopm̃o uidit ut un̄. stellas an̄ se cadente?

Et pea p diuersos montes ascendentes usq; loz
quedam lorndu et ab homunbz remotu ubi se
aurestarunt qui intellecta causa qua ibidem
neniat dirit eis scio nob locu adeo paratum.

Et eos non sine grandi labore ad locum ubi .vij.
stelle q̄s uidet in sompnio steterãt duxit et ait. hic
erit locus nester. ibi igitur ipo epō uiuo sēo nuuã
re edificare cepit pmã domū ordīs cartusiensiu.

Que domus cartusia uero nomine nuncupa
tur iuxta artos montes burgundie scdm illud iuo.
opidum in carcer est solitudo paradisus. pax
est in cella fons instant iuugia bella.

Quondie lacryme quondie gemitus et si quando
repugnate sompn oppsist: hnimo vix ossa lxxe
ca colidebant er cu scorpionu tm socius sepe cho
tis puellaru mirsse z sola libidinu mrendia

Quadā die leo claudicās monasteriū igressus
est ieronimi aut cum ceti fugent ĝi hospitio obui
at leo pedē ostdit ĝ z adhibita cura diligenti
liberatur et oi fentate ppolita inter eos habitat

Alia aūt ince auſtodiés aſinū leo ſompno quar̄
dormiuit aſinū pdit exſpge fuis uigies ſocui
nō repeut hinc ide q̄ur aſinū alonge ueniente
uidet cū camell q̄uos ad mōſteriū fuge cegit.

Huius aut̃ et alioꝛu penus paul9 pꝛitꝰ to
ma fugiẽs maria trãfiuit τ uaſtiſſima bẽuũ
peaꝛt ſecꝰ mare rubꝛũ p9 quod tẽpꝰ ãduni
mehoꝛe ſe lrꝛenin in coleꝛe edidtur i ſoṁ pꝛno

Que dum p silias anthoni' quereret ypoten
taturu obuia' ht qui e' dexta via ad paulu de
mostrat ide satiru repit siluax dru errore getuliu
et tande lupu q eum ad pauli cellam adduxit.

Cum aut̄ nō h̄ēret unde sepeliret aduenere leo
nes duo et foueā parāt septroꝗ; ad siluā redeūt
ā̄tioni aut tunicā. p. ex palmis ꝗ texta assūpsit
ꝗ i soleūbus utebat̄. āno dn̄i. ij. lxxx̄ septimo.

De sancto georgio ã.
C unn autem beat
georgius in no
mine dei martuum re

cepisset uenerunt ei pa
doæ regionis uiri excel
lentissimi et sanctum
corpus eius nocturno

um sanctus mar tans rex de celo audit
tir eustachius dicens confide eustachi
lugerit de filijs in uxore eris quippe recipimus
er filijs suis ab ipo salu uxorem letus cum filijs

Prudentes vir
gines aptate
lampades nestras ecce spő
sus nenit exite obuiam

ei. Versus.
Cadent a latere tuo
mille. Responsorium.
Et decem milia a dextri

Spes afflictis   salutis karole senior
timor hostibus   pia suscape uota tuor
tosta uiuis regula uir   Gloria et honore co
tutis tuus uia forma   ronasti eum domine.

quant nous enuoia
stes uir saint angle
gabriel a la uierge ma
rie dire et annunaer la
nouuelle et le conseil
de uir loy biau sur dieu
si comme ce fu uoir nõ
uueillies regarder en
pitie et nous doner uir
sainte misericorde. Am.
Pater nr̃ qui es icelis.

Doulx dieu
doulx pere
sainte tri
nite. j. dieu biau sur
dieu ie uous requiee
conseil et aide en ton
neur et a la remembrã
ce de celui hautisme cõ
sel que uous preuiste
de uir ppre sapience gr̃

enlumine mon cuer
a lui seruir et ame.
Dor maria graca.
Oraco. xv. ad bam
maria p gaudiu qd
huit i die assupois sue.

Cir fouule da
me pour pel
le grant ioie que no'
eustes au iour de ure
assumpaon quant
ure cher filz uous por
ta es aelx et nous co
ronna sur routes fe
mes du monde. dou
ce pries li pour mop
et pour tous pecheurs
et routes pecheresses
que pir sa digne puil
sance ilz aient nolete
disir lors de leur pechie

et de leur mes amen
dr. Aue maria gra.

Ad amprien
dam mam
suam m entu
domus. uille uel lou.

N mam pitis la
lutis et prospri
tatis dmgat do
mmus ihr xpt